HOT TOPICS

RAIDERS
AND INVADERS

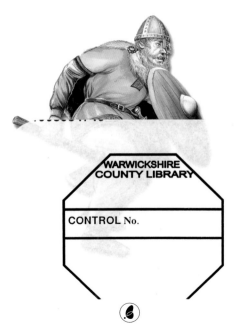

CHRYSALIS CHILDREN'S BOOKS

Useful internet websites

Check these out to find out more about warriors:

http://www.bbc.co.uk/education/anglosaxons/invasion/index.shtml
Here you can find out about the Saxons who invaded England 1500 years ago.

http://www.mrdowling.com/701-alexander.html
This site gives a full account of Alexander the Great's life and exploits as a warrior.

http://www.boglewood.com/timeline/attila.html
Follow Attila The Hun's journey of exploration and conquest from Italy.

http://www.bbc.co.uk/schools/romans/
Lots about the Romans and their army here. Try a quiz to see how much you can remember.

http://www.historyforkids.org/learn/medieval/history/earlymiddle/visigoths.htm
Find out about the Visigoths and other enemies of Rome, and scroll to the bottom
of the page to find out how to make a Visigoth crown.

http://www.mnh.si.edu/vikings/
Vikings sailed the North Atlantic too – find out about their journeys and the battles on the way.

http://www.nationalgeographic.com/genghis/
Find out more about Genghis Kahn and how he conquered such a large empire.

http://www.oldhistory.com/Unit8MiddleAges/Mi120.htm
Was there a children's crusade that ended in disaster? Read about what might have happened
and decide whether you think it's truth or legend.

http://www.elbalero.gob.mx/kids/history/html/conquista/noche.html
Read about the 'Sad Night' of the battle for Mexico and Cortés's defeat of the Aztecs.

http://www.discovery.com/stories/history/greatwall/greatwall.html
Take a tour along the Great Wall and find out how it was built to keep invaders out of China.

http://hazel.forest.net/whootie/stories/bruce_and_spider_body.html
Read the famous legend of Robert the Bruce and the spider.

http://www.net4you.net/users/poellauerg/Amazons/
Was there really a tribe of warrior women? Read about the legendary Amazons and decide for yourself.

Written by Rupert Matthews
Illustrated by Ed Org, Peter Bull, Mike Emden,
Alan Langford, Chris Rothero and Paul Colicutt
Designed by Kate Buxton
Cover designed by Clare Sleven
Editor: Rasha Elsaeed

This edition published in the UK in 2003 by
Chrysalis Children's Books PLC
64 Brewery Road, London N7 9NT

Every effort has been made to ensure none
of the recommended websites in this book is
linked to inappropriate material. However,
due to the ever-changing nature of the
Internet, the publishers regret they cannot take
responsibility for future content of these websites.

British Library Cataloguing in Publication Data
for this book is available from the British Library.

ISBN 1 903954 76 2

Printed and bound in China

Contents

What is a warrior? **4**

Who was Alexander the Great? **6**

Who was Atilla the Hun? **8**

Were the Romans warriors? **10**

Who did the Romans fight? **12**

Was Ireland warlike? **14**

Who were the Vikings? **16**

Who was Genghis Khan? **18**

What were the Crusades? **20**

Who were the Aztecs and Incas? **22**

Who was Sitting Bull? **24**

What is the Orient? **26**

What is a freedom fighter? **28**

Are all warriors real? **30**

Index **32**

What is a warrior?

Warriors were men or women who fought bravely. Often they were not paid to fight, but fought because they believed they were right.

Warriors did not win all of the time. Some of the most famous warriors are those who lost, but who fought with great courage.

Byrhtnoth was an English earl. In 991, he and all his men died fighting a Viking force near Maldon in Essex. They fought so bravely that a poem, called 'The Battle of Maldon', was written about their heroic struggle.

Shaka was the king of the Zulu, a large tribe in South Africa. In 1816 Shaka trained the Zulu warriors in new battle tactics. By 1850 the Zulus had defeated all neighbouring tribes. In 1879 the Zulus wiped out a British regiment before being defeated by the British at Rorke's Drift and Kambula.

Warriors used different types of **weapons**. Early warriors used clubs and rocks, while more modern warriors used rifles and cannons.

The **Assyrians** conquered a large empire in the Near East about 3,000 years ago.

Ashanti warriors fought in the dense forests of West Africa about 100 years ago.

The **Maori** live in New Zealand. They used to live in great tribes which fought wars with each other, and later, with European settlers. Sometimes whole tribes were killed in battle as they refused to surrender. Although the Europeans accepted the Maori as equals in 1840, wars continued for many years.

Who was Alexander the Great?

In 336 BC Alexander the Great became King of Macedonia (in northern Greece). He was only 20 years old. Within 13 years he had become the most powerful ruler in the world.

He defeated armies larger than his own using clever new tactics and weapons.

Alexander's horse was called **Bucephalus**. According to legend Alexander, who was only 12 years old at the time, was the only person who could control him. When Bucephalus died Alexander named a town in India, Bucephala, in honour of him.

The Battle of Gaugamela in 331 BC was Alexander's greatest victory. He defeated a Persian army of 150,000 men with his army of only 35,000 Macedonians. The battle was won when Alexander led a cavalry charge which scattered the Persian infantry.

The cavalry led the attacks in battle. They were used to open gaps in the enemy army. The horsemen would charge forward, followed by the infantry.

King Darius was Alexander's biggest enemy. He became ruler of the Persian Empire in 336 BC after murdering the previous three rulers. Darius was a successful warrior who defeated many enemies, but he lost two major battles to Alexander. In 330 BC Darius was murdered by his cousin.

Infantry in Alexander's army used a very long spear called a **sarissa**. Each sarissa was 4.5 metres long.

In 323 BC Alexander's Empire was the largest in the world at that time. He wanted to join all the kingdoms he had conquered to form one country. After Alexander died, his generals divided the empire between themselves. Within 150 years the empire no longer existed.

Macedonia Black Sea

Greece

Battle of Gaugamela

Battle of Hydaspes

Syria

Persia (Iran)

Alexandria

Egypt

Arabia (Saudi Arabia)

India

Arabian Sea

The Empire of Alexander the Great

Alexander reached **India** in 326 BC. He defeated a local king, Porus, at the Battle of the Hydaspes (modern day Jhelum) and added new territories to his empire.

Who was Attila the Hun?

Attila was the king of the Huns, a warlike tribe feared in Europe and Asia. He became sole King in 444 after murdering his elder brother, Breda, who was joint King at the time.

Attila organised the Huns into a powerful army. By conquering neighbouring kingdoms he built up a large empire. Soon, he became known as 'the scourge of God'.

The Huns came from central Asia in about 370 and settled in what is now Hungary. Attila led his tribe in wars that ranged across Greece, southern Russia, Germany and France.

The Huns loved gold – during one raid into Greece they stole over 1,000 kg!

In 453 Attila died suddenly after a feast on his wedding day. He was buried with his treasure. The slaves who buried him were all killed to keep the location secret. Without Attila's leadership, the Huns were easily defeated by their enemies.

Attila arrived in Italy in 452 and captured many cities. Pope Leo I persuaded him to spare Rome from attack.

Venice is a city in northern Italy surrounded by the sea. It was founded by Romans fleeing from Attila. The escaping Romans were safe on the islands of Venice as the Huns did not have a navy.

Horses were the Huns' most important possession. They used them to look after their large herds of cattle and sheep. They also fought on horseback, using spears and bows to attack their enemies.

Hun warriors scarred their faces with knives to make themselves look fierce to frighten their enemies.

The Huns used the **lasso** as a weapon. One Hun would catch an enemy with a lasso, allowing another warrior to kill the captive.

Were the Romans warriors?

The Roman Empire began around 753 BC and lasted over 1,000 years until AD 476. It covered all the lands around the Mediterranean, and much of Europe.

These lands were conquered and policed by the Roman Army. The Romans defeated many enemies because of their superior weapons and tactics.

The Romans were excellent builders as well as warriors. They made roads to move their armies from one place to another, and built forts and walls to keep out invaders. **Hadrian's wall**, in northern England, was built to keep enemies from invading England from Scotland.

The legionary was the most important type of Roman warrior. Legionaries wore strong suits of armour and fought on foot. They were grouped together in a century, made up of 80 legionaries led by an officer known as a centurion.

Roman legionaries marched and fought together in a large group of 5,200 legionaries called a **legion**.

Horatius was a legendary early Roman warrior. In about 670 BC a large Etruscan army (from northern Italy) attacked Rome. The bridge leading to Rome across the River Tiber had to be cut down to stop the Etruscan invasion. Horatius fought the Etruscans single-handed to give the Romans time to cut down the bridge. Rome was saved and Horatius survived to be declared a hero.

Mark Antony was a famous general. He fell in love with Cleopatra, the Queen of Egypt, and gave her land belonging to Rome. This led to a civil war with the Roman authorities which Mark Antony lost. Later, he took his own life.

Legionaries arranged themselves in special formations when attacking the enemy. The 'tortoise' protected legionaries from arrows and spears. The 'wedge' was used to smash through enemy ranks.

The tortoise formation

A bronze eagle was the symbol of a legion and it was carried into battle. Romans thought it was an insult to the Gods if the eagle were captured by the enemy.

Who did the Romans fight?

The Roman Empire was very large and had many enemies. There were tribes fighting their Roman conquerers, and armies from other empires trying to invade Rome.

The **Celts** were divided into many different tribes, who lived right across Europe from Scotland to Serbia. They were often a war-like people, who rode chariots into battle and sometimes sang as they fought. After a battle, the Celts would cut off the heads of their dead enemies and hold a feast to celebrate.

Hannibal was a famous nobleman from Carthage (in modern day Tunisia). He was one of Rome's most dangerous enemies. In 218 BC he led his army, along with 38 elephants, from Spain through France and across the Alps into Italy. He won many battles there, including the defeat of 50,000 Romans at Cannae. He never reached Rome and was forced to return to Carthage.

Vercingetorix was the Celtic leader of Gaul (modern day France). He fought against the Roman general Julius Caesar in 52 BC. After several battles, Vercingetorix was captured and beheaded.

Spartacus was a slave who escaped from a gladiator school in 73 BC. Thousands of other slaves ran away to join him. Spartacus led them through Italy, stealing and burning everything they could find. He was defeated and died in battle at Lucania in 71 BC. The 6,000 prisoners captured by the Romans were all crucified.

Boudicca was Queen of the Iceni, a tribe from East Anglia, in England. In AD 61 she led her tribe in revolt after she and her daughters had been ill-treated by the Romans, who had also increased the taxes. Boudicca's Celtic warriors destroyed Colchester, London and St Albans before being beaten by the Romans. Rather than surrender, she poisoned herself.

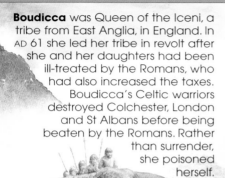

Arminius was a German chief. In AD 9 he and his warriors trapped three Roman legions in a swampy forest and killed them all.

Masada was a fortress in Palestine held by 1,000 Jewish rebels in AD 72–73. After a two-year siege by 15,000 Romans, all but seven of the Jews, including the children, committed suicide rather than surrender.

Was Ireland warlike?

Ireland was never conquered by the Romans. Instead, Ireland remained a land ruled by Celtic chiefs.

Although there was a High King of Ireland most tribes continued to fight each other.

Irish kings and chiefs often lived in well defended **strongholds**. The remains of the Rock of Cashel in County Tipperary are a good example of an ancient Irish stronghold. The rock was home to the kings of Munster.

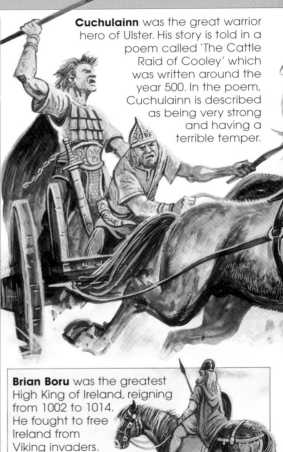

Cuchulainn was the great warrior hero of Ulster. His story is told in a poem called 'The Cattle Raid of Cooley' which was written around the year 500. In the poem, Cuchulainn is described as being very strong and having a terrible temper.

Brian Boru was the greatest High King of Ireland, reigning from 1002 to 1014. He fought to free Ireland from Viking invaders. He was murdered by a fleeing band of Vikings after finally defeating the Viking army at Clontarf.

Women are important characters in Irish mythology. The legendary **Queen Maeve** of Connaught led an army against Ulster, and fought against Cuchulainn.

Fionn mac Cumhaill was the legendary hero of Leinster. According to the stories told about him, he led a band of brave young warriors who loved to hunt. These warriors were known as the Fianna. The Fianna rebelled against Cairbre, High King of Ireland, in an argument about hunting lands. The Fianna were destroyed in the following battle.

Strongbow was the nickname of Richard Fitzgilbert, a Norman lord. He came to Ireland in 1170 to help Dermot MacMurrogh, King of Leinster, become High King. After Dermot's death, Strongbow grabbed his lands for himself. Soon, other Norman and English knights came to Ireland and took over much of the country.

Who were the Vikings?

The Vikings came from Norway, Denmark and Sweden. They raided northern Europe and even travelled to North America and Italy.

A carved head from a Viking ship

The Vikings were also merchants, trading with Arabs and people from Asia. They sold furs, ivory and slaves and bought silk, spices and gold.

Weapons were made by skilled craftspeople. Axes and swords were favourite weapons. Valuable swords were passed from father to son. They were given frightening names such as 'blood-sucker' or 'man-killer'!

Raids were carried out by warriors in longships. As many as 100 longships would take part in a single raid. The Vikings would land, capture as much money, food, cattle and valuables as possible and sail away again.

Longships were narrow boats which could be up to 30 metres in length. They were not very heavy and were very quick through the water as they had oars as well as a large sail. Some longships had dragon heads carved on to them to make them look fiercer.

Sweyn Forkbeard was the greatest Viking of his time. He built a large empire based around the North Sea. He was King of Denmark and Norway, and in 1013 he became King of England.

The Vikings started to settle in the places that they had raided in the past. There were **settlements** in northern England, northern France and southern Ireland. Remains of these settlements can still be seen in York, in England, and Dublin, in Ireland.

Eric Bloodaxe became King of Northumberland, in England, in 948. He had been forced to flee from Norway after murdering two of his brothers to become sole King of Norway. Eric was driven out of England in 948, and again in 954. He was killed later that year on returning to England.

Viking warriors believed that when they died they would go to **Valhalla**, the banquet hall of the gods. Viking chiefs and famous warriors would often be buried with their boats and their favourite possessions when they died. Sometimes the body would be placed on the deck of the boat and burned.

Who was Genghis Khan?

Genghis Khan united all the Mongol tribes of central Asia and created the largest land empire the world has ever seen.

His empire relied upon ferocious mounted warriors and a reign of terror, which left cities burnt to the ground and millions of people dead.

Each warrior had two bows, 100 arrows, a lance and a sword. Arrows came in several designs. Some were specially shaped to travel long distances, others to pierce metal armour. One type of arrow was fitted with a whistle to frighten enemy troops.

Genghis Khan's real name was **Temujin**. He was born in 1167, the son of a minor tribal chief. His father was poisoned by a neighbouring tribe, and Temujin became leader himself. He acted very bravely in battle and at a meeting of the Mongol tribes in 1206 he was given the title 'Genghis Khan', which means 'Great Ruler'.

Genghis Khan was also the ruler of the **Merkit**, **Tartar**, **Kirghiz** and **Naiman** tribes.

The Mongols were a very ruthless tribe. When they captured a city they would put women, young children and the craftsmen who made weapons to one side. Then they would kill everybody else. When the city of **Merv** was captured, about 700,000 people were killed.

The invasion of **China** began in 1211 when the Mongols broke through the Great Wall. In 1215, Peking was captured and northern China was conquered.

The Mongols fought on horseback. Their horses were small and strong. They were bred to withstand the cold and heat and were trained to keep calm in battle.

The **Mongol Empire** was the largest land empire ever known. By 1279 it stretched from Hungary to Korea and included most of Asia.

Russia

Arabia

China

India

Pacific Ocean

Arbian Sea

The Mongol Empire

What were the Crusades?

The Crusades were wars between Christians and Muslims. There were seven Crusades between the years 1095 and 1300.

The name 'Crusader' comes from the Latin word for cross. The Christian warriors were called Crusaders because they wore a cross as their badge.

Assassins were sent into Crusader camps by the Muslims to murder important leaders.

Richard the Lionheart was a King of England who led the Third Crusade in 1190. At the battle of Arsouf, in 1191, Richard defeated a large Muslim army and in the following year, he defeated another Muslim army at Jaffa. He led the Christian attack himself and acted with great bravery. Richard forced the Muslims to agree to a truce that allowed Christians to visit Jerusalem.

Warrior monks fought in the Crusades. These were special monks who made promises to God to fight against the Muslims. The Templar Order was the most famous group of warrior monks. The order was founded in 1118 to protect pilgrims going to Jerusalem. Other orders included the Hospitallers, the Trufac and the Teutonic.

Saladin was the great Muslim leader of the 1100s. In 1175, he became Sultan (ruler) of Damascus and went on to unite the Muslims. He defeated the Crusaders in many important battles and stopped them taking over Jerusalem.

El Cid was the nickname given to Rodrigo di Vivar. He was a great Spanish warrior who fought against the Muslims. El Cid means 'The Champion'. In 1094 he defeated the Muslims and captured the city of Valencia. He ruled it until his death in battle in 1099.

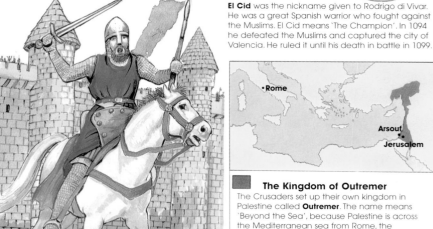

The Kingdom of Outremer

The Crusaders set up their own kingdom in Palestine called **Outremer**. The name means 'Beyond the Sea', because Palestine is across the Mediterranean sea from Rome, the Christians' headquarters.

21

Who were the Aztecs and Incas?

The Aztecs were a warlike people who lived in Mexico. By 1450, they had formed a large empire stretching from the Pacific Ocean to the Caribbean.

Aztec Empire

Inca Empire

The Incas came from Peru. Their empire covered an area four times as large as France. The Incas believed it was their holy duty to conquer other tribes and make them worship the Sun God.

The Aztecs and Incas used weapons made from wood with sharp polished pieces of a rock called **obsidian** set in them to make a cutting edge.

In 1423 Pachacuti, the Inca ruler, ordered work to start on the fortress of **Sacasahuaman**. The fortress had three massive towers and three walls made of stone. The walls were in a zigzag shape. The stones were specially shaped to fit into each other like pieces in a jigsaw.

Every Aztec man joined the **army** at the age of 17. If he had not performed a brave act by the age of 23, he had to leave the army to become a farmer or merchant. Very brave warriors were allowed to wear special animal skins.

Spanish troops, known as **Conquistadors** (meaning conquerors), attacked the Aztecs in 1519, and the Incas in 1532. The Conquistadors rode horses into battle and were armed with steel swords and guns. These modern weapons were too powerful for the Aztecs and Incas, and both their empires were conquered.

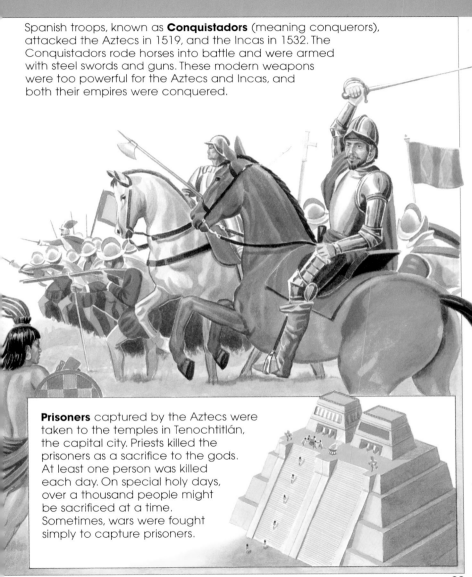

Prisoners captured by the Aztecs were taken to the temples in Tenochtitlán, the capital city. Priests killed the prisoners as a sacrifice to the gods. At least one person was killed each day. On special holy days, over a thousand people might be sacrificed at a time. Sometimes, wars were fought simply to capture prisoners.

Who was Sitting Bull?

Sitting Bull was the greatest leader of the Sioux people. He united the Sioux tribes.

With the help of the Blackfeet, Cheyenne and Arapahoe tribes, he led a war against the American settlers.

Warriors like the Sioux fought on horseback. They were armed with spears, bows and arrows, or guns bought from the white settlers.

The **first Indian War** began in 1608 when English settlers fought the Powhatan tribe in Virginia. The war ended in 1613 when the Indian princess Pocahontas married an Englishman.

Red Cloud was chief of one of the Sioux tribes. He fought against the American army to stop them from building forts and a road across land belonging to the Sioux and Cheyenne tribes. The war lasted for two years, from 1865 until 1867, when the government was forced to leave the tribes' land. Red Cloud made peace with the settlers, but continued to defend the rights of his people with many visits to the government in Washington.

When **gold** was found on Sioux land, the American government ordered Sitting Bull to move his people to a new reservation 380 km away. Sitting Bull refused to move and war broke out between the government and the Sioux.

In 1876, General Custer was sent with the 7th Cavalry to attack the Indian camp at **Little Big Horn**. Custer sent part of his troops to attack the Indian rear, and charged forwards with the remaining troops. He rode straight into a trap set by Sitting Bull and another chief, called Crazy Horse. Custer and all his men were killed.

Geronimo was the leader of the Apache, who lived in the deserts of the USA-Mexico border. In 1859, the Apache were attacked by Mexicans. After this the Apache fought a war against all whites. For many years Geronimo led his warriors in a brutal conflict until he surrendered in 1886.

What is the Orient?

The Orient is the name given to the lands to the east of the Mediterranean Sea, especially those in eastern Asia, such as China or Japan.

Many ruthless warriors have fought each other across this vast area of land.

Samurai warriors came from Japan. They were highly-trained fighters who were loyal to their local lord. All Samurai followed a strict set of rules, known as Bushido. These rules encouraged the Samurai to be brave, honest and live a simple life. If a Samurai broke the rules of Bushido or lost a battle, he had to kill himself. This was known as seppuku.

The **Great Wall of China** was built by the Emperor Shih Huang-ti around 220 BC. It was designed to protect China from invasions from the north. It is over 6,000 km long and wide enough to drive a chariot along the top. Today it is a major tourist attraction.

Early Chinese armies were made up of large numbers of peasants. They fought on foot as only the nobles could afford chariots or proper weapons. By 200 BC the Han Emperors had introduced cavalry. An example of what warriors looked like at this time can now be seen at Xian in China after the discovery of 6,000 life-size terracotta models of the Emperor Shih Huang-ti's army.

Timur the Lame, or Tamerlane as he was known in Europe, was the ruthless leader of the Tartar warriors from southern Asia. He was born in 1336 in Samarkand, which is in modern-day Tajikistan. By 1399, he had conquered or made treaties with all of central Asia, and invaded Russia and India. Timur was a cruel person who slaughtered thousands of people. He would build great pyramids of skulls from the people he killed before taking their treasure back to Samarkand.

An Lu-Shan was a Turkish warrior who became ruler of China. As a young man, he was a cavalry commander in the Chinese army. He won many victories against the enemies of China and was soon commander of the entire northern army. In 756, thinking the Emperor had ordered his death, An Lu-Shan attacked China. He overthrew the Emperor and became ruler of China. He was murdered one year later by a servant.

What is a freedom fighter?

Freedom fighters are warriors who try to free their country from the rule of a foreign nation.

Most freedom fighters work in small groups rather than with a large army. Sometimes they win and their country is freed. Other freedom fighters fail but they become heroes and inspire others to follow their ideas.

Joan of Arc led the French in a war against the English. In 1429 England ruled most of France. Joan, a young farmer's daughter, persuaded the Dauphin (the French heir to the throne) to let her fight with a small army. Joan amazed the troops with her bravery and leadership. She was captured and executed by the English in 1431. Thousands of French people were inspired by Joan and within a few years France was free.

Simon Bolívar fought to free South Americans from the Spanish Empire. In 1810 Venezuela threw out the Spanish Governor. Bolívar took command of the rebel army and won many victories. In 1821 Spain accepted defeat. Bolívar then went on to lead rebels in Colombia, Peru, Ecuador and Bolivia.

Francois Toussaint L'Ouverture was a black slave who led the slaves of Haiti to freedom. In 1791 he led a slave revolt against the foreign rulers of the island and by 1797 he was ruler of Haiti. Toussaint outlawed slavery and brought in many humane laws.

Giuseppe Garibaldi led a small group of followers to try and unite Italy. In 1860 Italy was made up of a large number of small kingdoms and much of the country was controlled by Austria. Garibaldi led just 1,000 men (called the 'Redshirts' due to the colour of their clothes) to Sicily. He began a revolution and swept northwards overthrowing many rulers. After only six months most of Italy joined together under the rule of the King of Piedmont.

Robert the Bruce led the Scots against the English. In 1296 Edward I of England was crowned King of Scotland. Robert the Bruce, a great grandson of an earlier Scottish king, claimed that he should be King. For years he was unsuccessful, until the Battle of Bannockburn in 1314, where the English army was smashed by Robert's Scottish troops. Scotland was a free nation again.

Are all warriors real?

Mythical warriors appear in legends from many countries.

Although fantastic stories are told about these warriors, the legends are often based upon the lives of real people.

Horus was an Ancient Egyptian god. It is thought that the many stories told about his conflict with the god Seth refer to ancient tribal conflicts before the first pharaoh united Egypt in about 2800 BC.

Gilgamesh was a legendary hero of Ancient Persia in about 2000 BC. In the legend, Gilgamesh is a king who goes on a long journey to try to discover the meaning of life. It is thought that Gilgamesh was a famous warrior-king of Uruk in about 2500 BC.

The Ancient Greeks and Persians told stories of female warriors called **Amazons**. The Amazons were a race of war-like women who raided other countries to capture gold and men. In fact, the Amazon legend was probably based on a real-life tribe called Sarmatians, who lived near the Black Sea between 800 BC and 300 BC. Sarmatian women had equal rights with men and fought in battles. This seemed very strange to the Greeks and Persians of the time and led to the stories about the Amazons.

Jason was a prince from Thessaly in Greece. Storytellers would tell tales of how Jason had to visit many distant countries with the help of a band of warriors called the Argonauts before he could be king. The stories are probably based on the journeys of several different Thessalians. Sailors from Thessaly visited many countries in search of trade.

King Arthur is a legendary warrior of Britain. According to legend, Arthur was a great king who led a band of noble and gentle knights. The knights sat around a round table so that no one would appear to be more important than any of the others by sitting at the head of the table. In fact, Arthur was probably a Celtic warrior who fought against the Anglo-Saxons (who invaded Britain after the Romans left). He is thought to have been killed at the Battle of Camlann in about 515.

Sigurd was a great hero warrior of the Vikings. He was the last of the Volsung tribe and had many adventures, like fighting a dragon and finding treasure. Nobody has been able to discover who the character of Sigurd was based upon.

31

Index

Alexander the Great 6–7
Amazons 30
Americans 24–25
Anglo-Saxons 31
An Lu-Shan 27
Antony, Mark 11
Apache 25
Arab 16
Arapahoe 24
Arc, Joan of 28
Argonauts 31
Arminius 13
Arsouf, Battle of 20
Arthur, King 31
Ashanti 5
Assassins 20
Assyrians 5
Attila the Hun 8
Aztecs 22–23

Bannockburn, Battle of 29
Blackfeet 24
Bloodaxe, Eric 17
Bolívar, Simon 28
Boru, Brian 14
Boudicca 13
British warriors 4
Bruce, Robert the 29
Byrhtnoth 4

Caesar, Julius 12
Cairbre, High King 15
Camlann, Battle of 31
Cannae, Battle of 12
Celts 12, 14
Cheyenne 24
Christians 20–21
Cleopatra, Queen 11
Conquistadors 23
Crazy Horse 25
Crusaders 20–21
Cuchulainn 14
Custer, General 25

Darius, King 7

Edward I, King 29
El Cid 21
English warriors 4, 15
Etruscans 10

Fianna, The 15

Fionn mac Cumhaill 15
Forkbeard, Sweyn 16

Garibaldi, Giuseppe 29
Gaugamela, Battle of 6
Geronimo 25
Gilgamesh 30
Great Wall of China 19, 26

Hadrian's Wall 10
Hannibal 12
Horatius 10
Horus 30
Hospitallers 20
Huns 8–9
Hydaspes, Battle of 5

Iceni 13
Incas 22–23

Jaffa, Battle of 20
Jason 31
Jerusalem, City of 20–21

Kambula, Battle of 4
Khan, Genghis 18
Kirghiz 18

Little Big Horn, Battle of 25

MacMurrogh, Dermot 15
Macedonians 6
Maeve, Queen 15
Maldon, Battle of 4
Maori 5
Masada 13
Merkit 18
Merv, City of 18

Mongols 18–19
Muslims 20–21

Naiman 18
Normans 15

Pachacuti 22
Persians 4–5
Pocahontas 24
Porus, King 5
Powhatan 24

Red Cloud 24
Redshirts 29
Richard the Lionheart 20
Rock of Cashel 4
Romans 10–14
Rorke's Drift, Battle of 4

Sacasahuaman 22
Saladin 21
Samarkand, City of 27
Samurai 25
Sarmatians 30
Scottish warriors 29
Seth 30
Shaka 4
Shih Huang-ti, Emperor 26
Sigurd 31
Sioux 24–25
Sitting Bull 24–25
Spartacus 12
Strongbow 15

Tamerlane 27
Tartar 18
Templars 20
Temujin 18
Tenochtitlán 23
Teutonic 20
Timur the Lame 27
Toussaint L'Ouverture 28
Trufac 20

Valencia 21
Valhalla 17
Venice, City of 8
Vercingetorix 12
Vikings 4, 16–17
Vivar, Rodrigo di 21

Zulu 4